HOUNDS
LOYAL HUNTING COMPANIONS

BY BECKY D. LEVINE

CONSULTANT:
DONALD SMITH
MEMBER
AMERICAN HUNTING DOG CLUB

CAPSTONE PRESS
a capstone imprint

Edge Books are published by Capstone Press,
1710 Roe Crest Drive, North Mankato, Minnesota 56003
www.capstonepub.com

Library of Congress Cataloging-in-Publication Data
CIP information is on file with the Library of Congress.
ISBN 978-1-4296-9990-7 (library binding)
ISBN 978-1-62065-934-2 (paper over board)
ISBN 978-1-4765-1546-5 (eBook PDF)

Editorial Credits
Angie Kaelberer, editor; Kyle Grenz, designer; Marcie Spence, media researcher;
Jennifer Walker, production specialist

Photo Credits
123RF: Veronika Petrova, 14-15; Alamy Images: Bruce Tanner, 13, Itar-Tass Photo
Agency, 7, Juniors Bildarchiv GmbH, 27; AP Images: Jackson Citizen Patriot/J. Scott
Park, 23; BigStockPhoto: i4locl2, 22; Capstone Studio: Karon Dubke, 17; iStockphoto:
BambiG, 5, Ccolephoto, 8, nickhayesphotography, 1; Shutterstock: AnetaPics, cover
(front), 28, Anke van Wyk, 16, ARENA Creative, 24, Cindy Underwood, 11 (top left),
20, cynoclub, 26 (top), Dennis Donohue, 26 (bottom), Frantisek Czanner, 25, Laila
Kazakevica, 21, lightpoet, 18, Liliya Kulianionak, 4, Nata Sdobnikova, 19, Natalia D.,
cover (back), Neil Roy Johnson, 6, PardoY, 11 (bottom left), Sheeva1, 11 (bottom right),
sokolovsky, 12, Tootles, 29, Villiers Steyn, 9, Will Hughes, 11 (top right)

Printed in the United States of America in Stevens Point, Wisconsin.
092012   006937WZS13

TABLE OF CONTENTS

CHAPTER 1

HUNTING BY SIGHT AND SCENT

In the middle of the desert, a jackrabbit hops. A whippet sees the movement. Instantly, the dog races across the ground as its owner watches. The rabbit runs, but the whippet is too fast. In a few minutes, the dog has caught the rabbit in its mouth and killed it. The hunt is over.

Whippets use their good eyesight to hunt.

4

Many miles away, deep in a forest, a cottontail rabbit stops to nibble some grass. A bassett hound smells the rabbit's trail. The dog sniffs the ground an inch at a time, moving slowly toward the rabbit. The hunter follows. Hours later, the hound finds the rabbit. The dog lifts its nose and howls. The hunter takes over and shoots the rabbit. Together, the dog and hunter have caught their **quarry**.

Bassett hounds search for prey by scent.

These stories are very different, and so are the dogs. But both the bassett hound and the whippet are hounds. And both of them are excellent hunters.

quarry—an animal that is chased or hunted

5

People have used foxhounds to hunt for more than 500 years.

THE HISTORY OF HOUNDS

Hounds have been around for thousands of years. Pictures of hunting hounds have been found in ancient Egyptian tombs. The word "hound" used to mean any dog that hunted quarry. People in the Middle Ages (AD 400–1400) wanted different kinds of dogs for hunting different quarry. They began breeding dogs that ran fast and dogs that had a strong sense of smell. These dogs were the ancestors of today's hunting hounds.

Many people in Europe hunted foxes with dogs in the 1500s and 1600s. In 1650 Englishman Robert Brooke brought a pack of foxhounds to what is now Maryland in the United States. Over the years, other hounds arrived in North America. Some people say French General Marquis de Lafayette gave two bassett hounds to President George Washington after the American Revolution (1775–1783). In 1889 William Wade brought the first Borzoi hound from England to the United States. At that time, the breed was known as the Russian wolfhound. American breeders also developed new hound breeds, such as the Plott hound.

Borzoi hounds

SIGHT HOUNDS AND SCENT HOUNDS

Most hounds belong to one of two groups, sight hounds and scent hounds. Sight hounds have sharp eyes that spot quarry even when it's small or far away. Scent hounds have noses that can track any smell. They will follow a scent trail for hours or even days. Some scent hounds can follow scents across lakes and other still bodies of water.

DOG FACT

The bloodhound is probably the best-known scent hound. It is most often used to track people instead of hunting animals.

Most sight hounds are tall, thin dogs with long legs. Their slender bodies help them run fast as they chase quarry. Scent hounds vary in size, but they are usually heavier than sight hounds. Some scent hounds have short legs, which keep their noses close to the ground. Scent hounds such as the basset hound have long, floppy ears. These dogs swing their heads back and forth as they follow a trail. The ears pick up smells off the ground and bring them closer to the hound's nose.

Greyhounds and other sight hounds are fast runners.

SCENT HOUNDS

Breed	Quarry
American English coonhound	bears, boars, bobcats, mountain lions, opossums, raccoons, squirrels, foxes
American foxhound	foxes
Bassett hound	rabbits
Beagle	rabbits, hares
Black and tan coonhound	bears, boars, bobcats, mountain lions, opossums, raccoons, squirrels
Blue tick coonhound	bears, boars, bobcats, mountain lions, opossums, raccoons, squirrels
Dachshund	rabbits, badgers
English foxhound	foxes
Harrier	hares, foxes
1 Plott hound	bears, boars, bobcats, coyotes, mountain lions, opossums, raccoons, squirrels
Portuguese podengo pequeno	rabbits
2 Redbone coonhound	bears, boars, bobcats, coyotes, mountain lions, opossums, raccoons, squirrels
Treeing Tennessee brindle	bears, boars, bobcats, coyotes, mountain lions, opossums, raccoons, squirrels
Treeing Walker coonhound	bears, boars, bobcats, coyotes, mountain lions, opossums, raccoons, squirrels

DOG FACT

Some hounds are named for their quarry. Dachshund means "badger dog" in German. Kelb-tal-fenek means "the dog of the rabbit" in Maltese.

Plott hound

Redbone coonhound

SIGHT HOUNDS

Breed	Quarry
Borzoi	coyotes, jackrabbits, foxes
Greyhound	rabbits
Kelb-tal-fenek (pharoah hound)	rabbits
Rhodesian ridgeback	bears, boars, bobcats, coyotes, mountain lions, opossums, raccoons, squirrels
Saluki	coyotes, jackrabbits
Whippet	jackrabbits, rabbits

Rhodesian ridgeback

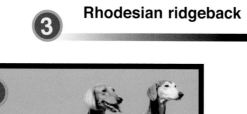

Saluki

11

CHAPTER 2

BORN to HUNT

Hounds are smart and independent. During a hunt, a hound doesn't wait for the hunter to tell it what to do. In fact, a hound doesn't even wait for the hunter to keep up with it. But hounds do have strong connections to their owners. They are happiest being part of a pack. To your dog, you and your family are its pack.

CHOOSING A HUNTING HOUND

When choosing a hound, think about the type of hunting you're going to do. Different hounds hunt different quarry.

Sight hounds are better at chasing fast animals. Scent hounds are good at slow tracking and hunting prey that climbs trees. Some scent hounds, such as the coonhound, see well at night. You can use this kind of hound to hunt nocturnal animals such as raccoons.

Treeing Walker coonhound

The place you live is also important when choosing a hound. When they're not hunting, sight hounds are usually calm and quiet. With enough exercise, they can be happy in an apartment or a small house. Scent hounds have a lot of energy and need plenty of space. Scent hounds also bark loudly. These breeds may be a better choice if you live in the country.

13

If your hound spends time in your yard, you must have a sturdy fence. When your hound sees or smells another animal, it will want to chase it. Invisible fences may not stop a hound on the hunt. You should build a covered wire mesh fence that is at least 5 to 6 feet (1.5 to 1.8 meters) tall. Hounds that are jumpers, such as salukis and coonhounds, may need an even taller fence. If your hound digs under the fence, you can reinforce the fence to keep it from escaping. Dig a deep trench and insert the fenceposts and wire mesh below the surface of the ground.

Whippets can have a strong prey drive.

Hounds, especially sight hounds, have a strong **prey drive**. Cats and other smaller pets may not be safe around them. But hounds raised with other pets are more likely to get along with other animals.

DOG FACT

The greyhound is the fastest dog breed. A greyhound can run 45 miles (72 kilometers) per hour.

prey drive—the urge to chase a smaller animal

PICKING A PUPPY

The best place to get your puppy is from someone who breeds hounds for hunting. Ask other hunters if they know a good breeder or contact a local hunting club. Then talk to the breeder about his or her dogs. Find out which puppies have parents or grandparents that are good hunters. You want a hound that comes from a strong hunting family.

Visit the breeder and ask to see where the dogs are kept. You also should meet your pup's parents, if possible. Spend time with a few puppies and play with them. Most puppies will nip a little, but don't choose one that bites or growls. This puppy may not get along well with you or with other dogs. Also, you don't want a puppy that appears shy. A puppy that is too timid won't be a good hunting partner.

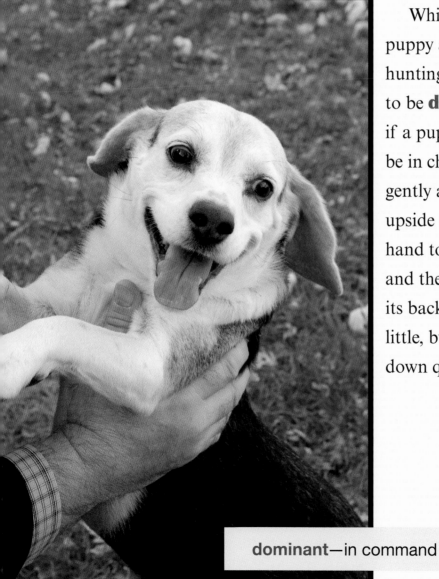

While you train your puppy and when you are hunting, you will need to be **dominant**. To see if a puppy trusts you to be in charge, you can gently and safely hold it upside down, using one hand to support its head and the other to support its back. It will squirm a little, but it should calm down quickly and relax.

dominant—in command

CHAPTER 3

TRAINING A HUNTING HOUND

Hounds have a strong hunting **instinct**. You won't need to teach your hound to go after quarry. But you should do some training to help your hound get ready for an actual hunt.

OBEDIENCE FIRST

Even though hunts are filled with noise and action, your hound will need to listen to you. The first commands your dog should learn should be "heel" and "whoa." When a dog heels, it sticks close by its owner when walking or standing. "Whoa" means the dog immediately stops what it's doing and focuses on you.

instinct—behavior that is natural rather than learned

When your hound follows your instructions, give it a reward. This reward can be a food treat or lots of petting. But the best reward of all is praise. Your dog wants to please you, and praise will tell it that it has done just that. If your hound does something you don't want it to do, correct it by simply saying, "No." Use a strong voice that lets the dog know its action isn't OK. Never yell at or hit your dog. You want a hound that loves being with you, not one that is afraid of you.

Your hound must return immediately on command.

The most important command for your hound to know is a recall command. The command may be your dog's name, a word like "come," or the toot of a whistle. When you use the command, your hound should return to you right away. This is especially important when hunting. A dog that fails to come when called won't be of any use to a hunter. It also could be a danger to itself or to others.

GETTING READY TO HUNT

Give your hound some practice time before taking it on a real hunt. Start your training in a small space. Your hound will have fewer smells and sights to deal with.

Let your hound get to know the sight and smell of the animals it will hunt. Make sure the training area has quarry in it. Take your greyhound to a field where rabbits live. Show your coonhound a few trees where you've seen raccoons. You can also use an animal **pelt** to train a scent hound. Drag the pelt across the ground for a short distance. This gives your young hound a short scent trail to follow.

pelt—the skin and fur of an animal

You can also take your pup on hunts with more experienced dogs. Many hunters and trainers say that older hounds make the best teachers for young dogs. Because the older dogs are dominant, your hound will follow and copy their behavior.

DOG FACT

If your pup doesn't seem interested in hunter training, wait a few days and then try again.

Foxhounds usually hunt in packs. The dogs work together to find prey.

ON THE HUNT

Hunting with sight hounds and scent hounds is very different. A sight hound performs almost every part of the hunt by itself. As soon as your hound sees the quarry, it is on the job. A sight hound chases its quarry, catches it, and kills it. The hunt is usually over quickly. Most sight hound hunters watch their hounds run from a distance or stay close in their car or truck.

When you hunt with a scent hound, you follow your dog as it tracks its quarry. A hunt with scent hounds can cover miles and may take several hours.

Scent hounds tree their quarry or trap it on the ground. The dogs bark loudly or bay to call their owners. When the hunters catch up, they shoot the quarry.

Tree Dog Training

Scent hounds such as coonhounds and Plott hounds often hunt by chasing their quarry up a tree. Raccoons are most often hunted this way. Because raccoons are nocturnal, the hunts take place at night.

On training hunts, take your hound to wooded areas where raccoons are likely to be, such as near cornfields, creeks, or lakes. Pick a night that doesn't have a full moon. Raccoons are more active on darker nights. Make sure the night isn't too windy. High winds can throw off a raccoon's scent.

Stay near your dog as it follows the scent. Once your hound finds the raccoon, it will bark and bay at the foot of the tree. That's your signal to shoot the raccoon or shake it from the tree. Don't let your dog attack the raccoon until it has more hunting experience. A frightened raccoon could easily injure a young dog.

CHAPTER 4

YOUR HOUND AT HOME

You and your hound won't hunt every day. Your dog is your pet as well as your hunting partner. You'll need to spend time caring for your hound at home.

Your hound should visit the vet at least once a year.

VET VISITS

As soon as you get your new puppy, take it to visit the veterinarian. At your first visit, ask your vet what food to give your hound and how often to feed it. The vet will also vaccinate your

dog against rabies and other diseases.

Your hound will spend a lot of time outside where it can pick up fleas and other pests. Mosquitoes that bite your dog can give it heartworms, while some ticks spread Lyme disease. Your vet can provide you with medicines that protect your dog from these pests.

HEALTH ISSUES

Hounds that eat too quickly can develop **bloat**. This condition can be fatal. To prevent bloat, feed your hound two or three small meals daily instead of one large meal. Also, wait two hours after a meal before exercising your dog.

Hunting hounds need food made for active dogs.

Some health problems are passed down to dogs through their parents or grandparents. Coonhounds, bassett hounds, and Rhodesian ridgebacks may develop dysplasia in their hips or elbows. Glaucoma and other eye problems are also sometimes seen in hound breeds. Ask your breeder about health clearances. These certificates prove that the breeder's dogs have been tested and cleared for these health problems.

bloat—a condition in which the stomach fills with gas

AFTER THE HUNT

Take care of your hound after each hunt. Your dog may run through grasses or across rough ground. Longhaired hounds such as the Borzoi and some dachshunds will need brushing after each hunt. Look at the pads of your hound's feet and between its toes. Make sure it hasn't cut itself on a stick or a rock. Use tweezers to remove any ticks from your hound. If the skin around the tick bite is red or becomes infected, take your dog to the vet.

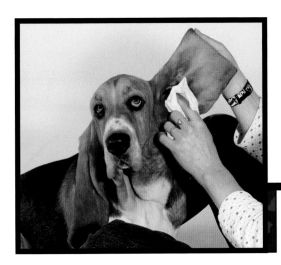

Regular ear care is part of owning a hunting hound.

Some grasses have sharp points called foxtails. Watch your dog for a few days after hunting. If it shakes its head often or rubs a paw over its nose or ears, it may have a foxtail in there. It's also a good idea to check your hound's ears after hunting. An ear that looks red or smells bad may be infected. If you think your dog has a foxtail or an infection, it's time to visit the vet.

Many hounds enjoy exercising at dog parks.

EXERCISE AND PLAY

Make sure your hound gets enough exercise. An overweight dog is not healthy and may have trouble keeping up on a hunt. Some hounds are eager to get outside and run. Others will be happy to lie around inside and wait for you to bring the leash. Either way, you should take your hound on one or two walks or runs every day.

You'll also want to socialize your dog. It's common for hounds to hunt together. A dog park is a good place for your hound to play with other dogs and get exercise. You can also take your hound for a run on the beach or play games in the backyard. The more time you spend with your dog, the better friend you'll have.

Some hounds participate in lure coursing competitions.

Hounds in Sports

Some hound owners enter their dogs in sporting competitions. These hounds compete in events that test their speed, endurance, and hunting ability.

Sight hounds do well at lure coursing events. Dogs chase a mechanical rabbit or other lure across a course that may include jumps or obstacles. They receive points for speed, agility, and ability to follow the lure.

Scent hounds can compete in tracking events where they follow a scent trail. Depending on the dog's experience, the trail may be fresh or several hours old. Dogs receive points for their ability to stay on the trail.

GLOSSARY

bay (BAY)—a deep, long howl

bloat (BLOWT)—a dangerous condition in which the stomach fills with air or gas and can become twisted

dominant (DOM-uh-nuhnt)—being in a position of command in a relationship

dysplasia (dis-PLAY-zhah)—a condition in which an animal's elbow or hip joints do not fit together properly

glaucoma (glahw-COH-muh)—an eye disease caused by pressure in the eyeball

infection (in-FEK-shuhn)—an illness caused by germs or viruses

instinct (IN-stingkt)—behavior that is natural rather than learned

nocturnal (nok-TUR-nuhl)—being awake and active at night

pelt (PELT)—the skin and fur of an animal

prey drive (PRAY DRYVE)—the urge to chase another animal

quarry (KWOR-ee)—an animal that is chased or hunted; also called prey

READ MORE

Crosby, Jeff, and Shelley Ann Jackson. *Little Lions, Bull Baiters & Hunting Hounds: A History of Dog Breeds.* New York: Tundra Books, 2008.

Gagne, Tammy. *Speaking Dog: Understanding Why Your Hound Howls and Other Tips on Speaking Dog.* Dog Ownership. North Mankato, Minn.: Capstone Press, 2012.

Landau, Elaine. *Dachshunds are the Best!* The Best Dogs Ever. Minneapolis: Lerner Publications, 2010.

INTERNET SITES

FactHound offers a safe, fun way to find Internet sites related to this book. All of the sites on FactHound have been researched by our staff.

Here's all you do:

Visit *www.facthound.com*

Type in this code: 9781429699907

Check out projects, games and lots more at
www.capstonekids.com

INDEX